MEET THE DISNEY BROTHERS

MEET THE DISNEY BROTHERS

Aaron H. Goldberg

QUAKER SCRIBE PUBLISHING
PHILADELPHIA, PA

MEET THE DISNEY BROTHERS

The book is not authorized, sponsored, or endorsed by the Walt Disney Company or any of its subsidiaries. It is an unofficial and unauthorized book and not a Disney product. Mentions of names and places associated with Disney and its affiliated businesses are not intended in any way to infringe on any existing copyrights or registered trademarks of the Walt Disney Company but are used in context for educational and journalistic purposes.

The author and publisher are not affiliated with or representatives of the specific companies, organizations, or authorities in this book. The opinions and statements expressed in this book are solely those of the people quoted and do not reflect the opinions and policies of the specific companies mentioned.

While every precaution has been taken in the preparation of this book, neither the author nor the publisher assumes responsibility for errors or omissions.

ISBN Hardcover: 978-1-733-64201-9
ISBN Paperback: 978-1-733-64200-2
ISBN ebook: 13: 978-1-7336-4202-6

Library of Congress Control Number: 2019901450

Cover design by Rob Yeo Design
Interior book design by Sue Balcer, Just Your Type.biz

First printing 2019

Published by Quaker Scribe Publishing
Philadelphia, Pennsylvania
quakerscribe@gmail.com

Visit the author on the web: www.aaronhgoldberg.com
Follow Aaron Goldberg on Twitter at @aaronhgoldberg

Table of Contents

Introduction

You have probably heard the word *Disney* before. Come on, who hasn't? Maybe you've visited Disneyland in California or Walt Disney World in Florida.

Perhaps you watch the Disney Channel on television or visit the Disney Channel on YouTube. Maybe you listen to Radio Disney. Wow, that's a lot of Disney!

Did you know there were two brothers with the last name of Disney who actually created this entertainment empire? You have probably heard of one of the brothers—his name is known around the world: Walt Elias Disney, better known as Walt Disney.

Did you know Walt used to wet the bed when he was a little boy? Yep, this is a true story. What makes matters worse is Walt had to share a bed with his older brother Roy! Roy enjoyed sharing this story from time to time when the brothers had become successful businessmen in Hollywood.

Roy and Walt were not only brothers but also best friends and business partners. Both men were creative geniuses in their own right. While Walt enjoyed stardom in front of the camera, Roy preferred to stay in the background away from the glamour of Hollywood, which is probably why you don't hear much about him. But today, you're going to learn a lot about Roy. This book is primarily about

Walt Disney, but his story can't be properly told without Roy and the strong bond between the brothers that propelled them to fame and fortune.

Roy excelled at being a businessman; he controlled the finances of the company and helped make all of Walt's dreams come true, the financial ones at least. Like most siblings, the Disney boys didn't always get along and had their share of fights and disputes. Once they even stopped talking to each other for nearly two years. But through thick and thin, the brothers stuck together and created some of the most famous characters, the most visited theme parks, and some of the most watched movies in the entire world, and it all started back in Chicago in June of 1893.

Chapter 1
Farm Boys

Walt and Roy's parents were Elias and Flora Disney, who lived in Chicago, Illinois. Elias worked as a carpenter and built the house the Disney family lived in. Flora was trained as a schoolteacher.

When the Disneys had their first child, Herbert, Flora left her job to care for her growing family. Soon a second child, Raymond, was born, and next came Roy on June 24, 1893. Eight years later, Walt was born on December 5, 1901. The fifth Disney child, Ruth, was born two years after Walt.

Shortly after Ruth was born, Elias began to think Chicago was changing and a big city wasn't a peaceful place to raise his family. Elias wanted his family to enjoy a wholesome life surrounded by nature. So in 1906 the family moved to a farm in Marceline, Missouri.

The Disney brothers loved life on their forty-five-acre farm. There were creeks to swim in and all the apples, peaches, and plums a boy could eat from their orchards. Best of all for Walt were the animals! He loved to play with the cows, chickens, and pigs. He even had a favorite horse named Charlie.

One of Walt's jobs on the farm was to take care of the pigs. He would often hop on the back of one of the critters and try to ride it. He usually fell off and landed in mud!

Well, one spring day Walt wasn't in the mood for a pig ride. As he walked around the farm he noticed a bucket of tar with a brush in it. Elias had used the tar to patch the holes in the farmhouse roof. Since the weather was warm, the tar was soft and could be spread like paint. Walt grabbed the brush and started to paint a picture of farm animals on the side of the white barn.

Just as Walt was finishing up his picture, he noticed his father walking toward the barn. Oh boy, Walt was in trouble now. Elias couldn't believe his eyes and questioned Walt about what he had just done. Elias tried over and over, but he was unable to get the tar off the barn. Walt received a big punishment that day. Unfortunately, it wasn't the first time he was punished by his father.

Elias was a very strict and religious man. He believed in hard work and in little fun and few games. Even at age six, Walt was very playful, creative, and silly. When he started elementary school, he was one of the class clowns. Walt loved to act and perform for his

classmates. These were all things Elias frowned upon and couldn't understand.

According to Elias, art and performing was for the wealthy, and the Disney family certainly wasn't wealthy. He thought his son should be more serious and refused to encourage Walt's artistic abilities and creativity. But there was another family member who encouraged Walt and hoped he would follow his heart and dreams: his Aunt Margaret.

About a week after Walt painted the picture on the side of the barn, his Aunt Margaret came to visit. While she didn't approve of the location of his artwork, she did think he had some artistic talent and thought Elias and the family should encourage him. Elias disagreed—there was too much work to do on the farm and Walt shouldn't be fooling around.

Aunt Margaret disagreed with Elias. On her next visit to the farm, she brought Walt colored pencils and pads of paper. Walt sketched anything and everything he saw. One day all of his sketching around the farm paid off.

Doc Sherwood was the town doctor. Good old Doc would let Walt come with him when he visited some of his patients. The two rode through town on Doc's horse. One day after Doc finished seeing his patients, he asked Walt to make a drawing of the horse.

Walt was excited but very nervous to make the drawing. He looked up to Doc and wanted to do the best job he could. As Doc held the reins to the horse to keep the stallion still, Walt sat down on Doc's front porch and quickly started to sketch the beautiful animal.

After a few minutes, the drawing was complete. Walt nervously handed over the sketch to Doc. "Walter, that's excellent! You know something? That's such a good picture, I'm going to frame it and hang it in my office. And you know something else? I believe a man should be paid for his services. Not just in hams and bushels of corn, the way I get paid sometimes, but in good cold cash. That's why I'm going to pay you five cents for this drawing."

Wow! What a great day for Walt. Another person appreciated his artwork, and this time he was even paid for it!

Unfortunately, a few years later, Walt had another memorable experience with Doc Sherwood. Only this time it wasn't as joyful. When Walt was about nine years old, his father became sick and Doc came over to check on him.

Walt listened outside of his father's bedroom door as Doc talked to Elias. According to Doc, the Disney farm was too large and required too much work. The family's two oldest sons, Herbert and Raymond, had left home and no longer helped out. Elias thought he could manage the farm himself with help from Roy and Walt.

When the brothers weren't helping on the farm, they went from door to door throughout the neighborhood, selling the fruit and vegetables the farm produced, while Flora pitched in and sold butter. But the family never had enough money.

Doc urged Elias to sell the farm. Another year of hard labor could kill him. The farm was too much work and not very profitable. A few days later, Elias sent Roy and Walt into town to hang up a stack of cardboard signs. The signs announced the sale of the farm. The Disney family was moving back to a big city.

On the day the farm went up for auction, Roy and Walt watched with sadness as their home for nearly six years was sold, along with all of their animals. Later that day the brothers went into town. Roy looked down the street and saw one of their favorite horses that had been sold earlier at the auction. The horse was tied to a buggy. As the Disney brothers continued down the street, the horse recognized them. He started to whine and buck, trying to get their attention. With tears in their eyes, the brothers went over and hugged the horse one last time.

Chapter 2

Kansas City, Here We Come

Elias hadn't been a very successful carpenter in Chicago when Walt was born. As the family experienced, he failed as a farmer too. Elias was determined to be a success in his next business as a newspaper deliveryman for the *Kansas City Star*. With the sale of the farm, Elias purchased a delivery route of 700 subscribers. He was in charge of making sure these readers received their papers each day.

When Elias sold the farm in 1910 and told the family they were moving to Kansas City, Missouri, Roy consoled his sad little brother by saying that life in the city would be easier. Sure, the boys had their share of fun playing on the farm, but farm life was a lot of work. Roy didn't think they would have to work as hard in Kansas City.

The brothers were looking forward to becoming more involved in school activities. Roy was going to be a senior in high school. Walt was still in elementary school. Roy could join a few sports teams, and Walt could continue with his art and maybe even get involved in his school's plays. Unfortunately, Elias had different plans for his sons.

In those days, newspapers were the main source of information and news. People didn't have the Internet or even television to rely on. Folks across the country waited eagerly for newspapers to be delivered to their homes. One edition of the papers came out in the morning and another edition came out in the evening. That sure sounds like a lot of work for the person delivering them.

Elias wouldn't be able to deliver all of the newspapers himself—he would need help. Just like on the farm, he relied on his two sons to do the work. Walt and Roy woke up at three thirty in the morning to deliver the morning edition before they went to school.

In the heat of the summer or in the freezing cold of a blizzard, the brothers had to deliver a newspaper to nearly every home in their neighborhood. If they missed a house, they would get in big trouble with their father. Only after they were finished could they go to school.

As soon as the school day was over, it was back to work for Walt and Roy. They walked home from school and immediately picked up the batch of evening papers that needed to be delivered.

These long days were exhausting for Walt. There were times when he fell asleep on the porches of the homes he was delivering papers to. He napped from time to time as well while he sat at his desk in school.

Walt and Roy were having a tough time working the paper route and going to school. The worse part of it all was their father didn't pay them for all of their hard work. When the boys would complain about not receiving any money, Elias would tell them, "I buy your clothes and shoes, and the food you eat. That's how I pay *you* for your work."

The boys didn't think this was very fair and had to work odd jobs so they could have a little bit of money. During recess at school, Walt ran across the street to the candy store and helped out the owner. He swept out the store and unloaded the deliveries. The shopkeeper didn't always pay Walt in money; sometimes he got a free bowl of chili and beans, which was one of his favorite meals.

One day Walt noticed Roy had bought a new tie. Walt liked the tie and decided to wear it to school. He figured he would make it home from school before Roy, and his brother would never find out that he wore it. Well, that day Walt had himself a nice big bowl of chili at the candy store.

As he finished the bowl, he looked down and noticed that Roy's new tie was covered with his lunch!

Walt did get home before Roy that day and returned the tie to the closet. That night, Roy went out on a date. About half way through the evening he noticed his tie was stained with chili and beans. He figured Walt was up to his old tricks again!

Roy could never stay mad at his kid brother. Walt looked up to Roy, and Roy looked out for Walt. The bond between the two brothers grew stronger each day. Roy gave his kid brother the encouragement and support he needed, which he didn't receive from his father. When Walt needed money to buy more pencils and paper so he could continue drawing, Roy always found a way to get Walt what he needed.

Another common bond between the boys was their disappointment in some of their father's actions. They were both tired of working hard and receiving no money for it. The brothers loved their father, but they were frustrated and tired of him treating them so poorly. There really wasn't much Walt could do about it. He was still a young boy, so he tried to accept it. Roy, on the other hand, was older and had an option.

One morning, at about 2:00 a.m., Roy woke up Walt. Roy looked at his brother and told him he was leaving. Walt told him it wasn't time to deliver the papers yet, he could go back to sleep for a bit. Roy told him he wasn't talking about leaving for work but leaving for good. Roy had enough of working for his father—it was time for Roy to be on his own.

Walt was devastated and begged Roy to take him with him.

Roy told him he was too young; he had to finish school first. Roy told his brother to take care of himself, turned off the light, and left the house.

The next morning Elias and Flora were shocked and sad. Roy left the house in the middle the night without saying goodbye to his parents, just as the oldest Disney boys, Herbert and Raymond, had done.

For the first time in their lives, Walt and Roy were apart. This was a really sad time for Walt. No longer would he and his brother share the same bed, telling stories and making each other laugh before one of them fell off to sleep. Walt missed Roy's support and encouragement. It took a little while for Walt to get used to life without his big brother.

Continuing with his drawing helped take his mind off of Roy. Walt even convinced his father to allow him to take art classes on Saturdays at the Kansas City Art Institute. Walt finally had the chance to formally explore his creative side and learn some of the art techniques he had been looking for.

Walt wasn't the only one who missed Roy; Elias missed him as well. With Roy gone, there was one less person to deliver newspapers. Just like back on the farm, Elias grew tired and looked for another business. Elias sold the newspaper route and invested in a jelly factory in Chicago. It was time for the family to move again.

Chapter 3
Growing Pains

Elias sold the paper route in the middle of the school year. Walt was fifteen at the time, and the family thought it would be best for him to finish school and then meet them in Chicago.

Luckily for Walt, his older brother Herbert lived in Kansas City. Herbert agreed to watch after Walt until the school year ended. As school came to a close, Herbert asked Walt what he planned to do over the summer. Walt didn't have any plans and wasn't really looking forward to moving to Chicago.

Herbert suggested he become a news butcher on the railroad. Do you know what a *news butcher* is? No? Well, neither did Walt! He asked his brother for more information.

Herbert told him the news butcher is the boy who walks up and down each train car selling newspapers, magazines, soda, candy, and sandwiches. This job would be a great way for Walt to earn some money and see the country. Best of all, it was aboard a train. Trains had fascinated

Walt since he was a little boy. Now he had the opportunity to ride one every day.

The next morning Walt went into town and applied for the position. He got the job! Success! Walt got hired for two months. He was very proud of the uniform he was required to wear. It was very official looking: a blue suit with brass buttons and a shiny badge.

Walt's first day was long. The train he worked on went from Kansas City to Jefferson City, which was about an eight-hour trip. The train was crowded and the passengers were hot. Walt knew just what they wanted—cold soda and lots of it.

Toward the end of that day, most of his time was spent on the last two cars of the train. These cars were full of commuters, and Walt sold them dozens and dozens of sodas.

When he finished working those cars, he walked back to the front of the train. He thought about what a great first day he just had. He had sold so much soda he couldn't even keep track of it or how much money he had made.

As the train pulled back into Kansas City, however, he received some bad news. The stop just before Kansas City was Lee's Summit. At this station, after all of the passengers exited the train, the last two cars were detached. Well, all of the soda bottles Walt had sold, which were now empty, were on one of the detached train cars. But in order for Walt to be paid for his work that day, he needed to return the empty bottles.

All of that hard work for nothing! Walt didn't get paid that day since he wasn't able to return bottles. But he still loved his new job. Before he knew it, the summer was over, and it was time to move back in with his parents and start high school in Chicago.

In the fall of 1917, Walt entered McKinley High School. As the school year went on, Walt became less interested in academics and more interested in pursuing his art. He enrolled in evening classes at the Chicago Academy of Fine Arts. Some of his teachers were popular cartoonists for the local Chicago newspapers. The more cartoons Walt saw, the more he knew he wanted to be a cartoonist.

Walt started drawing cartoons for his school newspaper. His fellow students loved his work. World War I was a popular subject Walt often featured in his cartoons. As the war raged across Europe, many young men wanted to join the service and fight for their country. Walt was no different.

His older brother Raymond was in the Army, and Roy joined the Navy. His desire to enlist grew even stronger when, one day after school, he saw Roy in his sailor uniform. Walt took one look at his brother and proclaimed,

"Boy! You look great in that uniform! I sure wish I had one!"

Roy suggested he go and join. Walt replied that he tried to enlist in both the Army and the Navy, but both branches told him he was too young. That all changed one day when a friend told him about a Red Cross unit that allowed seventeen-year-olds to join. The unit needed ambulance drivers in France.

This opportunity sounded great. Walt was still only sixteen years old, but that was the least of his worries. Somehow he had to convince his parents to let him join the Red Cross. Elias immediately said "no." Walt begged and pleaded with his father, but Elias didn't cave to Walt's wishes. Elias refused to sign the passport application, but his wife did not. Walt's mom knew she couldn't stand in her son's way and expressed her feelings to Elias.

Flora signed the application so Walt could enlist. After the paperwork was complete, Walt had a little more work to do. He needed to become seventeen years old—and fast. Walt altered his date of birth on the paperwork. With one quick stroke, he changed his year of birth from 1901 to 1900. Walt was now seventeen years old, at least on the application!

By the time Walt reached France by boat, the war was over. His services were still needed though. He spent the next year driving an ambulance around France. He drove injured soldiers to the ships returning to the United States and transported supplies and important military personnel around the country.

As the months went by, there was less for Walt to do. With more time than work on his hands, Walt looked for a way to make a dollar, or in this case a franc, which was the name of the currency in France. Walt asked a fellow worker if he would like a *Croix de Guerre*, a French military medal for bravery. Naturally the young man said "yes."

Walt painted the colorful medal onto his friends' leather jackets for five francs. Instantly everyone was a war hero!

Walt spent nearly a year in France. He experienced life on his own and was able to learn some valuable lessons. Unfortunately he even picked up a new habit: smoking. But through the good times and bad times he experienced in France, Walt was still preoccupied with art and cartooning.

He couldn't shake it, so it was time to do something about it. He was going home, and he was going to pursue life as an artist.

Chapter 4
Let's Get Down to Business

Walt was back on American soil in 1919. When he arrived, he lived with his parents in Chicago for a brief time, but his father couldn't accept Walt's career choice of cartooning. Elias wanted Walt to work in the jelly factory. He offered him a job that would pay him twenty-five dollars a week. Walt thanked his father but turned him down.

Elias couldn't believe his ears. He was tired of hearing about art and cartooning. He thought those things made for a good hobby but were terrible choices as a profession. Elias was furious at Walt's decision, but there wasn't much he could do about his son's choice.

After his year in France, Walt felt like a mature and wise man, not a teenager. He knew what he wanted to do with his life, and no one, not even his father, would stand in his way. Walt wanted to become a political cartoonist at a newspaper in Kansas City.

Roy, who was now out of the Navy, was already living in Kansas City, working at a bank. The brothers hadn't

seen much of each other since Roy had left their house in the middle of the night. It was time for the Disney brothers to reunite.

Walt's idea of becoming a political cartoonist didn't make it very far. Both of the newspapers in Kansas City declined to hire him. Walt was discouraged, but he still needed a job. As luck would have it, he landed a job at the Kansas City Film Ad Company. Sure, it wasn't political cartoons, but he could officially call himself an artist.

The Kansas City Film Ad Company created cartoon commercials for movie theaters. The commercials played before the movies started. Walt loved his job; he couldn't believe he was getting paid forty dollars a week to combine his sense of humor with his artistic ability.

Walt even made a new friend, a co-worker with a funny name: Ub Iwerks. Ub was a young man like Walt. He was a great artist too, much better than Walt. The two men discussed the cartooning process they used at work. Walt

thought the process was outdated. He wanted to learn even more about cartooning and character movement.

Walt went to the library and checked out every book he could find on the subject. After reading these books, he decided to could come up with a cartoon of his own.

Meanwhile, back in Chicago, Elias faced defeat in the business world again. The jelly company he was working for, and in which he had invested large sums of money, went out of business. The president of the company was a crook and swindled Elias out of thousands of dollars.

Elias had no choice but to move again. He decided to move to Kansas City where his children were. With Elias back in town, the entire Disney family, with the exception of Raymond, was living in one small house—talk about cramped quarters!

While Elias tried to find work as a carpenter, Walt was busy working at the film ad company during the day and practicing his own cartooning at night. He borrowed a camera from work and set up a little cartoon studio at home.

It didn't take Walt long to figure out how to use the camera and to apply the new techniques he had learned from the library books. One night he asked Ub to come over and view his work.

Walt had created a short but very funny cartoon. He used some of the stories from the local news as his subjects. Walt made fun of Kansas City's mayor and some members of the city council. Ub liked what he saw. Walt told him he was going to try and sell a few of these cartoons to the local movie theaters in town.

Things were going great for Walt, but the same couldn't be said for Roy. Not feeling well, Roy went for an X-ray, which showed a spot on his lung. Roy was diagnosed with tuberculosis, a disease that usually attacks the lung.

It appears Roy contracted the disease while he was in the Navy. At the time, the treatment for the disease was isolation in a warm, dry climate. Roy was sent to a hospital in Los Angeles to recover.

Not long after Roy left, the rest of the family, aside from Walt, moved to Portland, Oregon. Walt was now alone in Kansas City. He rented a room in a house and continued to perfect his cartoons. Walt wrote weekly letters to Roy informing him of his progress and his plans to sell a few of his cartoons to local theaters. Roy responded with letters of support and often enclosed money to help his brother's dreams come true.

One day Walt made an appointment with the owner of three theaters in town. He wanted to show the owner his funny cartoons. Walt thought they would be great to show before the feature films. The theater owner sat down and watched Walt's production. The cartoon ended and the lights in the room went back on.

The man asked Walt if the cartoons were expensive. Walt replied, "No, sir. I can make them for thirty cents a foot." The man liked what he saw and told Walt he would buy as many as he could make.

Woo-hoo! Walt did it! He was so happy and proud. His father said he would never be able to make a living as a cartoonist, but here on his first try he sold his cartoons to the Newman Theatres. Walt was now not only an artist, but a business man too.

As Walt walked out of theater basking in his success, a thought popped into his mind: wait a minute. He had told the theater owner it would cost thirty cents a foot. Darn! The price he had just told the owner was his actual cost for making the cartoons—he had forgotten to include some profit!

Oh well, it was a start. Walt was in business for himself. He had proven his father wrong and was very excited for what the future had in store for him.

Chapter 5
Go West Young Man

Walt decided to call his cartoon films for the theater *Newman Laugh-O-Grams*. Even though the films weren't exactly profitable for him, they were well liked. Walt found a few more theaters who were interested in his cartoons. This time he made sure to include some profit in the price!

Walt's new business was going great, so he quit his job at the Kansas City Film Ad Company. Next, he hired his friend Ub as a cartoonist. The business grew rapidly, and before he knew it, he needed even more employees. The *Newman Laugh-O-Grams* also led to a new idea.

Walt wanted to create short cartoons based on popular fairy tales. He needed more money to make this concept become a reality. Walt approached his friends, family, and local businessmen to see if any of them wanted to invest in his new idea. They did, and he raised $15,000! Twenty-year-old Walt was now officially the president of his own company, Laugh-O-Gram Films.

The new company produced its first cartoon, *Little Red Riding Hood*. A company in Tennessee loved what they

saw. The cartoon was funny and full of imagination. The company offered Walt $11,000 for six cartoons, with another five to be made in the future.

Walt was feeling great about his new company. If people loved his *Laugh-O-Grams* cartoons, they would probably love the next idea he came up with. His new idea combined cartoons with a live actress.

In those days, cartoons were a relatively new concept. Everyone across the country loved them. Walt figured if people enjoyed the cartoons before the movies, and they enjoyed the live action films with real actors and actresses after the cartoons, maybe he should combine the two.

Walt realized he could film a young girl in front of a plain white background and then have his artists draw cartoon figures around her. The actress and the cartoons would come together as if they were interacting—it would be great! Walt called the series *Alice Comedies.*

As it turned out, there was an East Coast film distributor—a company that sells films to movie theaters across the country—that could be interested in Walt's new Alice

series. Walt and his crew got to work on the first cartoon. Unfortunately, things weren't going so well with the fairy tale cartoons he had sold to the company in Tennessee. So far he had only received $100 out of the $11,000 he was owed.

With very little money coming into Laugh-O-Gram Studio, Walt was now living in the studio's office, sleeping in a chair every night. As the studio got about halfway through production of the first cartoon in the *Alice Comedies* series, *Alice's Wonderland*, he received the news that the company in Tennessee that owed him money was completely bankrupt. Production of *Alice Comedies* had to stop.

Walt spent almost all of the studio's money producing the fairy tales, and since he didn't receive payment for them, his company was now bankrupt as well. He faced a large amount of debt and didn't know what to do or where to turn.

He wrote Roy a letter and told him the sad story: "I'm through in Kansas City. My money is all gone. I learned my lesson: I can't get into the movie business here. I've got to go to New York or Hollywood, where most of the movies are made. And when I go, I don't want to get into the cartoon business. There are too many headaches, and there is too much work involved. I want to make the ordinary kind of live-action movie."

Roy wrote back and told him to hang in there and not be so hard on himself. He told his kid brother it was time to leave Kansas City. Roy encouraged him to take the train out to Hollywood so the brothers could meet up again. Walt listened to Roy; he sold his camera, packed his bag, and took a train out to Los Angeles.

Chapter 6
The Making of a Star

Walt Disney arrived in Hollywood during the summer of 1923 with only forty dollars in his pocket. Arrangements were made for Walt to stay with his Uncle Robert, who already lived in town. Roy was still recuperating in a hospital just outside of Hollywood.

Walt was going to try to become either an actor or a director in Hollywood. He went from studio to studio, often times either sneaking into or talking his way onto the studio grounds. Walt hung out at the studios all day, every day, but he had very little luck breaking into the field.

Roy told his little brother that maybe he should get a job outside of the entertainment business. Walt wasn't interested in that, even though he was running out of money and often borrowed five bucks a week from Roy so he could pay his Uncle Robert rent.

Just when it seemed like moving to Hollywood had been a bad idea, Walt got a break. From out of nowhere, he received a letter from the East Coast film distributor who had been interested in the live-action *Alice Comedies* cartoons.

The distributor, Margaret Winkler, was still interested in his idea, and she said she would pay him $1,500 per cartoon. Wow! What a great opportunity. After failing in Kansas City, Walt now had another chance in show business. He knew he couldn't make the same mistakes he had last time. He needed help. Lucky for him, his older brother was nearby.

Walt was so happy; he rushed off to see Roy in the hospital and shared the great news with him. As always, Roy was happy to see his brother. But today was a bit different—he noticed Walt was practically bursting with excitement.

Walt told Roy about the letter. Roy was proud of his kid brother. When Walt mentioned Winkler was willing to pay $1,500 a cartoon, Roy smiled and said that was big money. He questioned Walt about how much it would cost to make each cartoon.

Walt said he had it all figured out: it would cost about $750 per cartoon, which meant there was a great profit.

Roy smiled and nodded with approval. Walt then told Roy he needed his help. It was pretty clear that Walt was very creative, and he could come up with fantastic and creative ideas, but when it came to the financial side of things, he wasn't very good.

Walt hadn't calculated any profit into the *Newman Laugh-O-Grams*, and he had spent too much on the fairy tales without receiving any money in return. Roy had always been a financial whiz. He had worked in a bank and was always able to save money, whereas Walt was always too quick to spend his. The brothers shook hands. It was official: the Disney Brothers Cartoon Studio was open for business. Now all they needed to do was raise the $750 to make their first cartoon.

Roy had about $200 saved, but they still needed over $500 to make the cartoon. Walt knew a bank would never lend them money. Roy figured he would ask their Uncle Robert. Robert viewed Walt the same way Elias did—he thought he was unreliable and too much of a dreamer. Roy knew about Uncle Roberts's views but figured he could talk him into giving the brothers a loan.

After Roy explained the situation to Uncle Robert, he actually agreed to provide the loan. With the money in hand, Walt went out, bought a used camera, and showed Roy how to use it. The brothers went to work on creating their first live-action cartoon.

Within no time, *Alice Comedies* was a hit, and Margaret Winkler ordered more cartoons. The Disney brothers' studio was growing. Walt created the cartoons, made up the stories, and directed the actresses, but he needed help. Walt had the perfect person in mind. He reached out to his old friend from Kansas City, Ub Iwerks.

Ub agreed to move to Hollywood so he could work at the studio. He was a better artist than Walt, and he could complete the work faster than Walt as well. From that point on, Walt drew less as Ub handled most of the studio's most important animation.

Things seemed to be going smoothly for the Disney brothers. Walt and Roy were living together in an apartment near the studio. But working together and living together would often take its toll on their relationship. One night after the brothers got into a fight over Roy's cooking, Roy figured that was enough of them living together.

He sent a message to his girlfriend, Edna, who was still living in Kansas City. It was time for the couple to

get married. Naturally, Walt was the best man. After Roy moved out of their apartment, Walt started to date a young lady named Lillian Bounds. Lillian worked at the studio, helping paint the cartoons. A few months after Roy's wedding in April, Walt and Lillian got married on July 13, 1925.

Life was going great for both Walt and Roy. They were both married, and they even bought houses next door to each other. Their business was booming. By 1927 the studio had made over fifty of the Alice cartoons. Margaret Winkler, the distributor, had also recently gotten married. Her new husband Charles Mintz started to run the company after they married.

Charles requested that the Disney studio come up with a new cartoon character. Walt had Ub sketch a rabbit. Charles approved the sketch, and Oswald the Lucky Rabbit was born. Oswald was a funny little critter, with long ears and a big smile, that got into trouble from time to time.

With the addition of Oswald, the studio needed a larger facility, so the brothers had a new studio built. With their new studio came a new name for their business. The studio was now known as the Walt Disney Studio, not the Disney Brothers Cartoon Studio. Roy was fine with the change, acknowledging that Walt was the creative force behind the studio. Roy was just happy the studio was busy and making money.

Just like the Alice cartoons, the Oswald the Lucky Rabbit cartoons were a success. After a year of making the Oswald cartoons, Walt and Lillian took a trip out to New York City to meet with Charles Mintz. Walt was proud of the work his studio was producing, and Oswald was a very popular cartoon across the country. Walt knew if he could receive a little more money to produce the cartoons he could make Oswald even better.

Walt's meeting with Charles didn't go well. In fact, it was an awful meeting. Not only did Charles refuse to pay Walt more money for the cartoons, he decided he didn't need Walt at all. Charles told Walt something shocking. Sure, Walt created the Oswald cartoons, but he didn't own

them. According to their contract, Charles owned the characters—Walt's studio only produced them.

Charles then told Walt he was going to make the cartoons himself. Since Walt was in New York, he was unaware that, while he had been there, nearly all of his employees back in California had quit and gone to work for Charles. Thankfully, Ub stayed loyal to the Disney brothers and didn't quit.

Walt was devastated: How could this be? He felt like Oswald had been stolen from him. But it was all right there in the contract. Charles Mintz, not the Disney studio, owned the rights to Oswald.

What were the brothers to do? Roy and Walt had so much invested in Oswald. They had built a new studio and hired more employees. Without a character to put into the Disney cartoons, the family business was now on the verge of bankruptcy.

It was a long train ride back to California for Walt and Lillian. Sure, it seemed like Charles Mintz played a dirty trick on the brothers, but there was nothing they could do about it now. Walt was a dreamer; he had been one since he was a little boy. But he wasn't a quitter. If he dreamed up a successful character once, why can't he do it again?

As Walt and Lillian made their way across the country, they brainstormed. Sure, *why not* another character? There were already popular cartoon cats, dogs, and, of course, a rabbit. Why not a mouse?

Walt often sketched mice when he was a boy on the farm in Marceline. He would watch them as they ran through the fields and dodged the plows as they went by. Even back in Kansas City, while Walt was working at the Laugh-O-Gram Studio, from time to time a little mouse would scamper out of his trash can and climb up his desk.

As the train rumbled on and Walt sketched out a mouse on a pad of paper, Lillian asked what he was going to call his new character.

"Mortimer," Walt said. "Mortimer Mouse."

Lillian made a funny face. She said that name didn't sound very good. He needed a different name. "How about Mickey?" she asked.

"Mickey Mouse it is!" he replied.

Walt couldn't wait to get back to the studio so he could bring Mickey Mouse to life.

Chapter 7
A Mouse Named Mickey

It was 1928, and Walt and Roy had been in business for nearly five years. Within those five years they had built so much, yet they lost it all so quickly. Oswald was gone and the bills were mounting. The brothers and Ub started all over again with their new character, Mickey.

Walt was determined to make Mickey Mouse a star—Charles Mintz wouldn't get the best of the Disney brothers.

Walt wanted Mickey to be unique. He wanted his mouse to look more like a person than any of the other animals in cartoons. Ub's sketch of the mouse had human hands wearing gloves. (The next time you take a look at Mickey, check out his hands. He only has four fingers, not five. It's easier and faster to draw them that way.)

Walt and Ub went to work creating their first Mickey Mouse cartoon. The story for the mouse's first adventure was similar to a big news story at that time.

Charles Lindbergh was the first pilot to fly a plane by himself across the Atlantic Ocean. Lindbergh left Roosevelt Field, just outside of New York City, on Friday morning, May 20, 1927, and landed Saturday night, May 21, 1927, in Paris, France. Lindbergh was a hero known across the world.

This sounded like a great scenario for Mickey Mouse. *Plane Crazy*, Mickey's first cartoon, featured the mouse as a pilot, much like the popular Charles Lindbergh. The cartoon was in black and white and, like every other cartoon in those days, it didn't have sound.

To Walt's disappointment, the cartoon wasn't a hit. It was previewed at a local Hollywood theater but didn't receive much interest. Walt figured he would try again, so he created another cartoon for Mickey Mouse. The second cartoon is called *The Gallopin' Gaucho* and, much like Mickey's previous cartoon, Walt struck out again.

Walt was discouraged and nearly out of money, but he knew Mickey Mouse could be a star. He had one last idea.

When Thomas Edison invented the movie, or motion picture, camera back in 1892, movies didn't have sound. All of that changed in 1927 when the movie *The Jazz Singer* was introduced with sound. The public couldn't believe their ears! People on the screen opened their mouths and you could actually hear them talk. The public called these movies "talkies."

Walt thought this was exactly what he needed for Mickey Mouse. The public would love it if his mouse could sing and talk. He went to work on the third Mickey Mouse cartoon, *Steamboat Willie*. In this cartoon, Mickey is a steamboat pilot. Walt specifically created the scenes to reflect and incorporate sounds and music.

There was one small problem with making a Mickey talkie. Walt had to go back out to New York City to record the music and sounds for the cartoon. The studio was already running low on money, and once he was out in New York City, the whole process took much longer than he had expected.

At one point Roy informed his brother that they had a lot of bills to pay and there wasn't enough money to cover them. Roy suggested that Walt sell his car. Walt loved that car—it was a beautiful convertible. But times were tough and they needed the money. Roy sold Walt's car for him so they could finish *Steamboat Willie*.

Finally, after more than a few headaches, the third Mickey Mouse cartoon was complete. Mickey Mouse was

a talkie! Walt supplied the voice for Mickey and Minnie—Mickey's female counterpart—and a handful of men provided sound effects. A full band brought it all to life.

Mickey Mouse in *Steamboat Willie* debuted on November 18, 1928, at the Colony Theatre in New York City. (This date, by the way, is officially known as Mickey Mouse's birthday.) Unlike the first two Mickey Mouse cartoons, *Steamboat Willie* was a *huge* hit.

Mickey was funny, adventurous, and brave. He was also the world's first cartoon with synchronized sound. The entire world went crazy for Mickey Mouse. As Mickey's popularity grew, and it grew really quickly, Mickey had his own comic strip, dolls, toys, watches, pencils, notepads, and candy. Mickey even had a fan club.

In the early 1930s, Mickey Mouse clubs began popping up all over the country. Millions of children got together on Saturday mornings at their local movie theater to celebrate all things Mickey. Mickey Mouse mania was in full effect.

What was next for Walt, Roy, and the world's most famous mouse?

Chapter 8
Colorful Cartoons and Dark Days

The Disney brothers finally had a successful character that they owned and controlled. Mickey Mouse was the most famous cartoon character in Hollywood. In fact, he was probably the biggest star in the world!

The brothers were starting to adjust to life as the father and uncle of Mickey Mouse. Not too long after Mickey became a star, however, Walt received some bad news. Ub was quitting his job at the studio to start his own cartoon company.

How could Ub do this? Walt was mad and hurt. Ub was so important to the studio. He was *the* man who drew the original Mickey.

Walt and Roy hadn't let Charles Mintz ruin their lives when he stole Oswald, and this situation would be no different. The Disney brothers stuck together just like they always did.

With Ub gone, the studio hired more animators to replace him. These new animators helped Walt with a new idea he had been working on. Mickey Mouse had sound, but he was still in black and white. Walt thought Mickey would look great in color, but the studio wasn't that advanced yet. They needed some more time and experimentation to figure out the coloring process.

The idea of Mickey Mouse appearing in bright, vivid colors was very exciting. Unfortunately for his creator, life at that moment wasn't very bright and cheerful. Walt was struggling mentally and emotionally. Sure, Mickey was a huge success, but the energy and emotions it had taken to make Mickey a star had brought Walt a lot of stress.

The past ten years, going back to his days in Kansas City, had left him very tired and overworked. He had gone bankrupt, lost Oswald, and now Ub was gone. To make matters worse, Walt and Lillian wanted to have a baby in the worst way, but up until this point, they were unable to have one.

Roy and his wife had a baby boy, Roy Edward, born on January 10, 1930. The little boy was the apple of Roy's eye. Walt was so happy for his brother and wanted to experience the same joy of being a father.

The stress of work and the thought of not being able to have a child sent Walt into a mental breakdown. For no reason he would start crying or become very emotional at any little thing. A doctor told Walt he needed a vacation.

Lillian and Walt went on their first vacation since they had gotten married. The couple went to Washington, DC, to visit the nation's capital. Then they boarded a train to

Key West, Florida, and took a cruise to Cuba. From Cuba, they crossed through the Panama Canal, and then went back home to California.

Walt came back from his vacation refreshed and relaxed. It was time for the studio to make cartoons in color.

Walt learned about a new process called "Technicolor." To purchase the process, he first needed to convince Roy that cartoons in color would be worthwhile.

After all of the years of struggle, the studio was finally financially stable, and Roy closely guarded the company money. He didn't want to see Walt waste any money, especially on a new process that may not work. But after a long discussion, Walt got his way. The company would move forward with Technicolor. Walt had the perfect project in mind to showcase this new creation.

After the success of Mickey Mouse, the studio developed another series of cartoons called *Silly Symphony*. These cartoons didn't feature a specific star like Mickey Mouse. Instead, each cartoon had a different story and subject. Walt thought he would experiment with color in the *Silly Symphony* cartoons.

The experiment paid off in 1932 when the *Silly Symphony* cartoon *Flowers and Trees* became the first animated film to win an Oscar at the Academy Awards. Over time, *Silly Symphony* introduced some of Disney's most popular stories: *The Three Little Pigs*, *The Big Bad Wolf*, *Mother Goose Melodies*, and *The Ugly Ducking*. Speaking of ducklings, the *Symphony* even introduced the world to everyone's favorite duck: Donald!

Audiences loved these Disney cartoons in color, and by 1935 Mickey Mouse was colorized too. Things were going great for Walt at the studio. Back at home things were very happy as well.

On December 18, 1933, Walt was at an award ceremony in Hollywood. About halfway through the ceremony he was notified that there was a family emergency and he must leave. Walt rushed out of the building and went to the hospital as fast as he could. Lillian was about to give birth to a baby girl, Diane Marie. Three years later, the Disney's adopted another daughter, Sharon Mae.

It seemed like everything had perfectly come together for Walt and Roy. They both had happy families, the studio was successful, and Mickey Mouse was delighting audiences in both sound and color. In addition, the studio had just perfected a new camera called the "multiplane."

With this new camera, the studio could create cartoons with different depths and dimensions. The multiplane camera split the field of view—the area visible through a camera's lens—into different planes or levels.

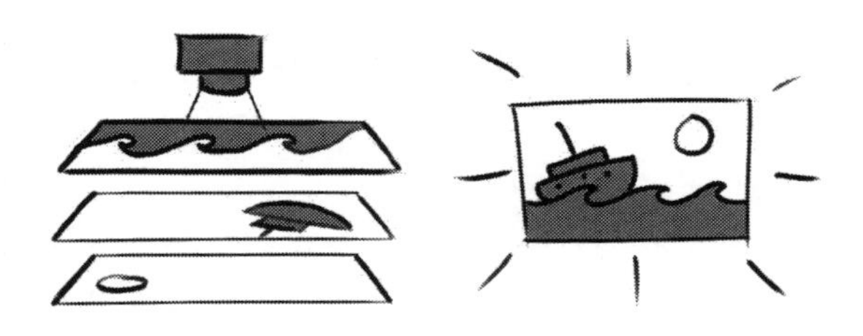

Separate levels are used for the foreground, middle ground, and background. The foreground is the view closest to you in a painting or photograph. The middle ground is in the middle of the painting or photograph, and the background is the scenery behind the main object in the painting or photograph. When each of these levels comes together on film, the scenes look real, three dimensional, and not flat.

Walt had the perfect project for the multiplane camera. When he was a young boy in Kansas City, he went to the theater and saw the fairy tale "Snow White." He had loved the story ever since.

One day Walt asked Roy if they could have a meeting. Roy knew what this usually meant—his brother needed money!

Walt started to talk about "Snow White." He told his brother it was the perfect love story. There was a villain, a hero, a princess, and a few funny little characters. This fairy tale was the perfect story to make a full-length cartoon, something no one had ever tried before.

The average Mickey Mouse or *Silly Symphony* cartoon was usually under eight minutes. Walt's version of "Snow White" would be ten times longer. Roy figured this would be a lot of work and would definitely cost a lot of money. More importantly, he wondered if people would be bored watching a cartoon for nearly an hour and a half. Walt was confident that people would love this cartoon.

One night he gave around fifty studio employees money for dinner. He told them to go across the street and eat. When they were finished, they were to come back to the studio and have a seat near the stage.

Once everyone returned, they saw Walt standing on the stage by himself. For the next three hours, Walt proceeded to act out the entire story of "Snow White," changing his voice to sound like the evil queen, Snow White, the

prince, and each dwarf. Walt painted a wonderful picture of the story in his employees' heads—he became each character right before their eyes.

When Walt was finished, his employees were amazed. They loved the story and were inspired by what they had just witnessed. At the end of the evening, he announced that they would be making this story into a full-length animated feature film.

Roy and everyone else in the room that night had seen Walt's passion and enthusiasm. Roy promised his brother the estimated $500,000 needed to make his dream a reality. Heigh-ho, Heigh-ho, it's off to work they go!

Both brothers knew there was a lot at stake with this production. Walt used the original fairy tale, as written by the Grimm Brothers, as a guide for his own version of "Snow White." In order to keep the audience interested for eighty-three minutes, Walt knew he needed more than just a love story. There had to be a lot of humor and personality as well—and this is where the seven dwarfs came in.

In some of the Grimm versions of the story, the dwarfs were named Blick, Flick, Glick, Snick, Plick, Whick, and Quee. Those names were terrible! What did they even mean? Walt decided their names should be based on characteristics that best described each one of them.

Some of the original names the studio came up with were Baldy, Wheezy, Deafy, Jumpy, Sniffy, Lazy, Puffy, Stubby, Tubby, Shorty, and Burpy. Those names weren't much better than the Grimm versions! And in fact, some of them were just mean!

After more work the names were finally set: Doc, Grumpy, Happy, Sleepy, Dopey, Bashful, and Sneezy. With the names set and the story complete, the animators went to work creating the hundreds of thousands of drawings needed to complete the cartoon.

Walt demanded perfection. There were days when he saw some of the artists' work and told them it wasn't good enough. He had them start over and recreate the scenes until Walt thought they were perfect, even though each redo cost the studio both more time and money.

One day Roy went to see Walt in his office. He looked Walt in the eyes and told him the studio was in trouble. Walt responded with a laugh and said, "We usually are!"

Roy told him he wasn't joking—the studio was running out of money and the banks wouldn't lend them any more.

Walt asked him what their options were. Roy said there was one last bank that could maybe help them out, but there was a catch. They wanted to see Walt's "Snow White" first. If they couldn't see what had already been done, they would not consider loaning Disney the money.

Walt hated to show an unfinished film. It was something he had never done before, but Roy insisted—they needed the money.

When the banker came to the studio, Walt showed him some of the film. There was no sound yet, only the cartoon, so much like he had done on the stage in front of his employees, Walt helped bring the story to life.

As the banker sat there watching Walt, he didn't even crack a smile or nod in approval. He didn't react to the jokes at all.

Walt finished, the banker stood up, and the two men walked back to the banker's car. Walt figured he had blown it; his heart sank in disbelief. The two men shook hands and the banker got into his car. Just before he pulled away, he looked at Walt and said, "You know Walt, that picture is going to make us a hatful of money." The bank loaned the studio the money it needed to finish the film.

The Disney brothers spent over $1.5 million dollars on the film, which was an enormous amount of money in 1937. As it turned out, the film was worth every single dollar.

Snow White and the Seven Dwarfs premiered on December 21, 1937, at the Carthay Circle Theatre in Hollywood. Walt Disney sat in the theater while the biggest stars in Hollywood watched his masterpiece. He heard them laugh, and he heard them cry, as the movie played on the screen. At the end of the evening, the audience roared with applause. His movie was a huge hit.

During the production of the film, most of Hollywood called the project "Disney's Folly." People didn't believe a

cartoon could be made into a successful full-length movie. Critics thought the brothers were crazy to invest so much money in it.

Not even six months after the debut of the film, the studio made so much money from *Snow White* that it completely paid off its bank loans. There was also enough money left over to start construction on a massive new studio in Burbank, California, which the company still uses today.

The brothers even splurged and bought their parents a house in Los Angeles. Elias and Flora left Portland, Oregon so they could be closer to their grandchildren and enjoy life as the parents of two of Hollywood's biggest moviemakers.

In 1938 Elias and Flora settled into their new house just blocks away from Roy's home. They were happy and enjoyed life in Los Angeles. Tragically, all of this happiness was short lived.

On November 28, 1938, the heating system in their house malfunctioned and deadly gas filled the home. Elias survived the accident, but unfortunately, Flora passed away from inhaling the fumes.

The brothers felt an enormous amount of guilt because they had bought the home. They were both heartbroken, and Walt never spoke about his mother again.

Chapter 9 Bombs

With the success of *Snow White*, Walt decided the studio should make more full-length cartoons. This time they would create their own cartoon versions of the popular children's books *Pinocchio* and *Bambi*.

The new Disney studio was turning into an animation factory, which was something the employees started to dislike. They were used to working in one large building, but the new facility in Burbank was split up into many buildings. Employees were separated by what type of job they performed. Many of the studio's workers started to feel isolated from one another. Before the move, they all felt like one big family—now, not so much.

The new studio was very modern; it featured air-conditioning, which was something most places around the country did not have. There were even underground tunnels that connected the buildings. These tunnels came in handy when it was raining. Workers wouldn't have to risk carrying the cartoons in the rain, which could ruin all of their hard work. As time went on, even these new studio features couldn't make everyone happy.

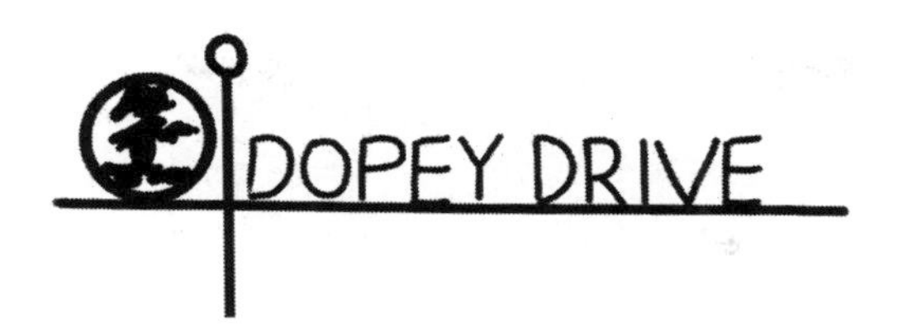

When Disney moved into the new studio, World War II—a major war in Europe—was taking place. The Disney studio had been making a lot of money off of their cartoons and movies being shown in European countries. Now, with the war taking place, there was only a little bit of money coming back into the studio. With profits down, Roy thought it would be best to decrease the workers' salaries so the studio could survive.

This made the workers furious. They complained and, eventually, went on strike in May of 1941. Walt felt like a father figure to many of his employees, so he couldn't believe they refused to work. Instead, they picketed outside of the studio and screamed and banged on his car as he entered each morning.

Walt was sad his employees felt this way and could act this disloyal. The situation became too much for Walt. The stress was making him sick; it was time for him to get away again.

Walt went on a trip to South America. Roy stayed back at the studio to work on bringing the strike to an end. Roy was successful in his negotiations and brought the employees back to work. Walt was happy to learn the strike was over. Unfortunately, a few weeks later, while Walt was still touring South America, Roy relayed some very sad news: their father had passed away.

In the summer of 1941, the Disney studio was preparing to release another animated feature. This one would be based on the book *Dumbo*. None of the movies Walt released since *Snow White* were very successful; they had all bombed. He and Roy were hoping *Dumbo* would be different.

By late fall *Dumbo* had become a popular movie, not nearly as popular as Snow White, but successful nonetheless. *Time* magazine was going to honor Disney's beloved flying elephant with the cartoon's portrait on the cover of one of the magazine's December 1941 issues.

All of that changed on December 7, 1941, when the Japanese military attacked Pearl Harbor, a US naval base near Honolulu, Hawaii. This surprise attack brought the United States into World War II.

Rather than featuring Dumbo on the cover of the magazine while the country was at war, a photograph of General Douglas MacArthur was published instead. In the days

following the attack on Pearl Harbor, the United States declared war on Japan, Germany, and Italy.

With the country involved in the war, things changed rapidly in the United States. One of the biggest changes for Walt and Roy took place at their studio. On the same day as the Pearl Harbor bombing, the United States Army took over the Disney studio.

The studio was the perfect location in which to repair army equipment and store ammunition. It was located near the factories where the Army's planes were built, and the Army needed to be close by to protect those facilities.

In addition to turning the Disney studio into a military base, the government asked the brothers to develop and create cartoons to help support the war effort. The studio created a series of training films for nearly every branch of the military. Some of the films taught the soldiers how to keep good hygiene or how to survive on a tropical island. Others showed them how to spot enemy airplanes or how to launch bombs.

The Treasury Department even enlisted Donald Duck—a star even more popular than Mickey Mouse at the time—to encourage people to buy war bonds and remember to pay their taxes.

When the war finally ended in 1945, the world was in bad shape. The Disney studio was no different. The studio had kept busy completing all of the films for the government, but they had made very little money.

Walt really wanted to move forward with more full-length animated films. But Roy didn't think that was a great idea. He told Walt that *Pinocchio*, *Bambi*, and *Fantasia*—a 1940 film featuring Mickey Mouse—had nearly left them bankrupt again. Roy put his foot down. He told Walt they didn't have the money to produce more full-length animated films.

Even though the Disney movies were finally being shown across Europe now that the war was over, no European country would allow any of the money made by the movies to be sent back to America. So, for the time being, the studio couldn't receive any of the profits it made in Europe.

Neither brother would back down on the subject of producing more full-length movies. Walt knew if he could just get Roy to give him the money to produce the feature film *Cinderella*, the movie would be a hit and save the day. Roy wasn't convinced. It would be better to save the money, or at least do a smaller project.

One evening the brothers finally had it out. Here's how Roy tells it:

> I remember one night he came down to my office, and we sat there from quitting time to eight or so. I finally said, 'Look, you're letting this place drive you nuts, that's one place I'm not going with you.' I walked out on him.
>
> I didn't sleep that night, and he didn't either. The next morning I'm at my desk, wondering what the hell to do. We were in a heck of a fix, tight payroll on our hands and everything. I felt awfully low. I heard his cough and his footsteps coming down the hall. He came in and he was tearing up, he could hardly talk. Walt says, 'Isn't it amazing what a horses ass a fella can be sometimes?' And he turned around and walked out. That's how we settled our differences. We put *Cinderella* into production.

Through thick and thin, and differences of opinions, the brothers always found a way to work it out. Even if they couldn't openly communicate, they both wanted what was best for each other and their company. Walt and Roy knew that to be successful family should always stick together and support one another.

As it turned out, Walt was correct. *Cinderella* was a huge success and made the studio a lot of money. And of course, yet again, Walt had another idea. This one would be his biggest yet.

Chapter 10
Disneyland Is Your Land

Ever since Walt lived in Marceline, a town created by the Santa Fe Railroad, he had a fascination with trains. In chapter three, you read about the summer he worked as a news butcher for the railroad. Now as an adult, he wanted to relive his life on the railroad.

Walt couldn't just quit the studio and go back to selling papers and soda on a train. So what was the next best thing? How about building his own railroad!

One evening Walt came home from the studio and told his family they were going to move. He was having a new house built, and he wanted to put railroad tracks and a train in the backyard. His two daughters and wife laughed and then screamed, "What?!"

Lillian asked what the neighbors would say.

"It won't bother them," Walt said. It wasn't going to be full size; it would be one-eighth the size of a real train.

His daughter Diane told him that men his age don't play with trains. That's for kids! Walt smirked. His daughter Sharon wondered what she would tell her friends if they

came over and saw her father playing with a train. Walt told her that he would give them a ride on it!

The women of the Disney house weren't too happy about Walt having a train in their backyard. But they had a wonderful father, and if this made him happy, even though they wouldn't ride on it, they would support him.

After about six months of construction, Walt's backyard had a half-mile railroad track, complete with a tunnel. He named the railroad the Carolwood Pacific, since they lived on Carolwood Drive. To keep Lillian happy, he named the locomotive after her: the Lilly Belle.

The more Walt rode on his railroad, the more he loved it and started to dream. What if he could have a bigger railroad? This dream actually worked well with another idea he had been thinking about.

On Sundays, Walt liked to spend time with both of his daughters. He would often take them to amusement parks around Los Angeles. One Sunday afternoon he came home and told Lillian about their experience. The park they had visited was awful. The rides weren't entertaining, the park was dirty, and things didn't seem safe. Worst of all, there was nothing for grownups and their children to do together. He had to sit on a bench and watch his daughters on the rides.

Walt thought he could make a much better amusement park. He started to share his thoughts and ideas with a few of the employees at the studio, but not directly with Roy yet.

Word often traveled fast around the studio. "Junior's got his hand in the cookie jar again." This was Roy's favorite line whenever he found out Walt had another big, expensive idea for the studio. This time it sounded like Walt had both hands in the cookie jar!

When Roy found out about Walt's new idea, he couldn't believe his ears. Walt knew nothing about amusement parks. When they finally talked about it, Walt reminded Roy about the small amusement park about a block from their childhood home in Marceline, and about Electric Park, a park they visited when they lived in Kansas City. They both had a lot of fun at those parks.

Walt was very detailed and passionate as he told Roy about his idea for an amusement park. He said it would even have a full-size railroad that went around the perimeter of the park, much better than the Carolwood Pacific.

Nope, no way—Roy was not getting involved in this, and he certainly wasn't going to find the money for Walt to complete the project. Little did Roy know, Walt had already started to raise money to make his dream park come true.

Walt borrowed money against his life insurance policy, which gave him around $100,000 to get started. Walt spent that money really fast. So he went to the bank and borrowed more. When Roy saw that Walt was spending his own personal money on the project, he finally realized that his brother was really serious. The brothers sat down to have another conversation about one of Walt's most expensive dreams.

Walt went into more detail about the park. He wanted "Disneyland" to be divided into several lands or mini-kingdoms where visitors could briefly escape from the present day. It would be a place where you could go to experience things from the past, and even "go into the future," experiencing what life could be like "tomorrow."

Roy saw his brother's passion, but he still thought it was a huge risk. Roy asked his brother how he was he going to finance Disneyland. Walt said one word: *television*.

In the early 1950s, television was a new form of entertainment. There weren't satellite dishes or cable TV. There were actually only three major networks. Yes, that's hard to believe! There was the National Broadcasting Company (NBC), the Columbia Broadcasting System (CBS), and the American Broadcasting Company (ABC).

Walt was always fascinated by television, and the television networks were always fascinated by him. They repeatedly asked him to create a show for their stations. Finally, in 1950, Walt accepted their offer, but just to produce a special one-off. On Christmas Day, Walt's first show on television debuted. It was called *One Day In Wonderland*. The special was a huge success. But Walt still didn't think he was ready for a consistent presence on TV.

Many movie industry leaders were afraid of television. They figured if people could stay at home and be entertained by TV, there would be no reason for them to go out to the movies. As the years went by, Walt began to think differently. He thought TV shows and movies could coexist, and TV could be the way for him to get his amusement park built.

Walt reminded Roy that the three television networks were interested in a regular Disney TV program. He told Roy to reach out to them; if one of them would help Walt finance the park, he would do a television program for that network.

Roy went to work. Many of the television executives he spoke with shared Roy's initial thoughts about the amusement park. They thought it was a terrible idea. But Roy believed in his brother and continued to pitch the idea. ABC was interested in putting Walt on television. The company agreed to a deal—Disneyland was coming to life.

The television show *Disneyland* premiered in October of 1954, just nine months before the Disneyland theme park was set to open in July of 1955. The show was hosted by Walt and featured exciting updates and previews about the Disneyland Park being built in Anaheim, California.

The television show also showed a variety of cartoons. Believe it or not, one of those cartoons actually helped the United States go into outer space—seriously!

The cartoon is called *Man in Space* and aired in March of 1955. The cartoon talked about rockets, satellites, and how man could survive in space. The studio hired actual rocket scientists to work on the project. The scientists provided the information and story to Disney so he could make the cartoon.

Over 40 million people watched *Man in Space*. After the cartoon aired on TV, United States President Dwight D. Eisenhower asked the Disney studio to send a copy of the cartoon to the White House for high-ranking members of the government to watch.

In July of 1955, President Eisenhower announced that the United States would launch its first unmanned satellite to orbit the earth. Years later, members of the National Aeronautics and Space Administration (NASA) acknowledged that *Man in Space* helped bring attention and interest to the space program and, eventually, launch a man into space.

Meanwhile back on earth, Disneyland was complete and ready for opening day. Walt thought this was another great opportunity for television. He arranged for ABC to broadcast the opening day festivities. Walt asked one of his friends, an actor named Ronald Reagan, to help host the show.

Decades later, Mr. Reagan went on to become the fortieth president of the United States, but on a really hot day in July of 1955, he was one of the hosts at Disneyland, which featured several never before seen lands of fantasy and adventure.

The park had Tomorrowland, which was supposed to resemble life in the future; Fantasyland, where you could visit with characters like Peter Pan and Sleeping Beauty; Adventureland, designed to feel like a tropical jungle; and Frontierland, which felt like the Old West of the 1800s, where cowboys ruled. All of these parts of the park still exist today!

Last, but not least, was Main Street USA. This part of the park is still located at the entrance of Disneyland and resembles Walt's hometown of Marceline, Missouri. Walt had

a secret apartment built over the firehouse on Main Street where he would often spend the night.

As families at home watched, and learned about Disneyland, they quickly fell in love with what they were seeing and couldn't wait to visit. But if you were one of the people who actually visited Disneyland that day, you most likely had a different experience than those watching on television.

The cameras didn't show the chaos in the park. Walt and Roy had planned that day, July 17, as a televised preview of Disneyland. They had sent out a few thousand invitations to the press, employees, family, friends, celebrities, and politicians.

Well, someone duplicated these invitations, and thousands upon thousands of counterfeit invitations spread throughout Southern California. Nearly 30,000 people showed up that day, and Disneyland was very unprepared for that amount of people.

The park ran out of food and drinks. The water fountains didn't work, there weren't enough bathrooms for people to use, and the asphalt sidewalks weren't fully dry yet. As women walked on the sidewalks, their high-heeled shoes sunk into the concrete and got stuck!

It sounds like a terrible experience, but most visitors didn't care. They loved the park!

Chapter 11

It's Hard to Say Goodbye

Disneyland was a huge success. The opening day problems were minor and the brothers fixed them immediately. On Disneyland's opening day, Walt said, "As long as there is imagination left in the world, Disneyland will continue to grow, to add new things."

Within weeks after Disneyland opened, Walt was up to his old tricks again. His imagination was working in overdrive. He wanted to get more money together so he could improve the park.

Roy commented that once Disneyland opened, it seemed like he never stopped writing checks. Walt didn't care about cost. He would say this needs to be done, that needs to be done, and again, he would demand Roy to find the money.

But Roy couldn't find the money to improve Disneyland just yet. The park was still new, and they still had a lot of debt. Instead, Walt went back to an old idea; he told Roy to explore making another television show. The money they would earn doing that could be used to improve Disneyland.

Again, Roy made a deal with ABC. They wanted an afternoon children's show to air Monday through Friday. Walt agreed and created *The Mickey Mouse Club*. The show debuted in October of 1955 and featured the Mouseketeers, a group of children who sang, danced, and performed skits.

Children across the US fell in love with the show. Nearly three-quarters of all television sets tuned in to watch the program between 5:00 p.m. and 6:00 p.m. every weekday. Walt was happy too; the money the show generated allowed him to add more attractions to the park.

The original show ran until 1959, and after a brief 1970s revival, *The Mickey Mouse Club* returned to television again in 1989. You may have heard of a few of the Mouseketeers from that show: Justin Timberlake, Ryan Gosling, Christina Aguilera, and Britney Spears, all who got their start on the show.

It may have been a struggle at times, but with the support of his loyal brother, Walt had conquered the world of family entertainment.

The brothers were getting older, they had both become grandparents, but that didn't mean they were going to slow down. By the early 1960s, Walt had three major projects in mind for the studio, two of which he was willing to share with the public—the other project was top secret.

His first project was to turn the book *Mary Poppins* into a movie featuring live action and animation. Walt's daughter Diane loved the book when she read it as a child. In 1944 Walt had Roy reach out to the author, P.L. Travers. He hoped to purchase the story from her so the studio could make it into a movie. Travers wasn't interested, but the Disney brothers never stopped trying to buy it.

Finally, in 1960, they were successful, and the studio went into production on the film. The movie premiered in August of 1964 and it was a box office smash. *Mary Poppins* received thirteen Academy Award nominations and became a popular movie for decades.

Just a few months before the film's debut, Walt was busy in New York City at the 1964 World's Fair, an exhibit of industrial, scientific, and cultural items from around the world. Visitors to the fair could try different foods, ride attractions, and learn about the different products being showcased.

Disney created four exhibits for the fair: *It's a Small World—a Salute to UNICEF and the World's Children*, at the Pepsi-Cola pavilion; *Progressland*, at the General Electric Pavilion; *Ford's MagicSkyway*, for the Ford Motor

Company Pavilion; and *Great Moments with Mr. Lincoln*, at the Illinois Pavilion.

The exhibits Disney created were the most visited attractions at the entire World's Fair. Walt figured these attractions were so successful, he could make a few changes to them and bring them back to Disneyland—he could even feature them at his new top secret project.

In 1965, local newspapers in central Florida reported that a mystery company, or companies, had bought large chunks of land near a sleepy little town called Orlando. Reporters couldn't figure out who had bought over forty-three square miles of land, primarily orchards and swampland.

As it turns out, Walt and Roy had bought the land. They didn't want the public to know it was them, or the price of the land would have really gone up. So they created fake company names to protect their identity and keep their project secret until they were ready to announce it.

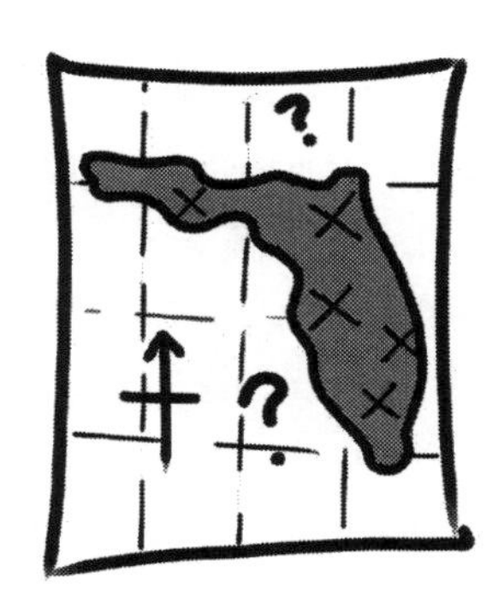

The brothers used names such as Latin-American Development and Management Corporation; Tomahawk Properties, Incorporated; Reedy Creek Ranch, Incorporated; Bay Lake Properties, Incorporated; and Ayefour Corporation. That last name, Ayefour, was actually a play on words. The major highway leading to the new Disney property was, and still is, Interstate 4, sometimes just referred to as "I-4." A pretty sneaky name for their company!

Eventually, the secret came out: Walt Disney was going to build a city of the future in central Florida. He was going to call it EPCOT, which stood for Experimental Prototype Community of Tomorrow.

EPCOT was going to be a place where people could live and work. It would be unlike anything else the world had ever seen. It would demonstrate and try out new ideas and systems for those living and working there. EPCOT would develop and grow as time went on and the country changed.

Walt felt like this was his true calling. He had been so successful on so many levels, and he felt like he could improve the American lifestyle. With the purchase of all of this land, he would dedicate the rest of his life to this project. Walt also wanted to include a version of Disneyland on the property in Florida.

With this project, time, not money, was Walt's biggest obstacle. With the success of *Mary Poppins* and Disneyland, Walt figured the company had enough money to get things started. Tragically, less than a year after the "Florida Project" was announced, Walt was diagnosed with lung cancer.

All of his years smoking, starting when he went to France with the Red Cross, caught up with him. In November of 1966, Walt went to the hospital for a check up. The doctors there discovered the cancer and admitted him to the hospital so they could operate on him.

Roy went to visit his kid brother every day while he was hospitalized. On the evening of December 14, Roy visited with Walt after work. As Walt lay in his hospital bed, he described his plans for their Florida project. He pointed to the ceiling and told Roy where he thought roads should go and what could be built around them.

Roy went home for the evening and told Edna he thought Walt had a good chance of making it through all of this. At nine thirty the next morning, just ten days after his sixty-fifth birthday, on December 15, 1966, Walter Elias Disney died.

Chapter 12
Dreams to Legacies

Walt became a regular face on television during the 1950s and 1960s. He was like a member of the family when he visited millions of homes each evening on TV. During this time he earned the nickname Uncle Walt. The world was shocked when they found out their favorite uncle had died.

As for Roy, he was never the same after his brother passed away. He didn't think Walt would die before him. For the first time, Roy had to lead the company by himself. The company he co-founded decades ago now had over 4,000 employees. Roy assured them that very little would change, and it would be business as usual.

Just prior to Walt's death, Roy was considering retirement. He was in his late sixties and thought maybe it was time for him to step aside. This was not an option now. He had a new task, one that meant more to him than just about anything else in his life—make sure his brother's last dream came true.

Roy wasn't sure if he could fully accomplish Walt's EPCOT dream. But he would certainly try. The first project

the company started on in Florida was the East Coast version of Disneyland.

Roy gathered the employees who were working on the project and told them, "We're going to finish this park, and we're going to do it just the way Walt wanted it. Don't you ever forget it. I want every one of you to do just exactly what you were going to do when Walt was alive."

Roy even decided on a name for the new park in Florida. It wouldn't be called "Disneyland Two" or "Disneyland East"; it wouldn't even be called "Disney World." Roy said it was going to be called "Walt Disney World," so everyone would be reminded of the creative genius who created the Disney company.

About a year after Walt's death, the company started construction on Walt Disney World. The theme park would be very similar to Disneyland, except it would be much larger. The Walt Disney World version Magic Kingdom—a fairy tale themed and Disney character inspired part of Disneyland—would feature many of the same attractions as the one in Disneyland, along with a few new ones.

At the center of the park would be the beautiful Cinderella Castle, which today stands at 189 feet tall. Roy knew people would come from all over the country to visit this new park so he had two hotels built, the Contemporary Resort and the Polynesian Village.

The Contemporary was designed so the monorail—a sleek-looking vehicle that rides along an elevated beam—would actually enter the hotel, pick up or drop off passengers, and then exit out of the other end. What a cool idea!

After several years of construction, and over $400 million dollars, Roy and his crew were able to transform orange groves and swampland into one of the most magical places on earth. On October 1, 1971, Magic Kingdom, the two hotels, two golf courses, and camping grounds opened to the public.

If you remember back to Disneyland's opening day, it was full of confusion and chaos. The same couldn't be said for Walt Disney World's. Opening day went off without a hitch! Just like Disneyland's opening ceremonies, however, Walt Disney World's was televised too.

Roy accomplished his brother's final dream. He brought Walt Disney World to life for the entire world to enjoy. At the end of opening day, Roy became nostalgic and reminisced about his life with Walt:

"My brother and I went into business together almost a half a century ago. And he really was in my opinion, truly a genius—creative, with great determination and drive; all though his entire life he was never pushed off course or diverted by other things. Walt probably had fewer secrets than any man, cause he was always talking to whoever would listen!"

Walt felt the same way about Roy. When he had the opportunity, usually during interviews about their company,

Walt would let the world know how he felt about his older brother:

"I had this brother eight and a half years older. I could go and talk to him and tell him things I could never tell my dad. My father never understood me. He was a wonderful man but very strict. I would tell my dad I was going to be an artist, he couldn't see it. But my big brother would say, 'Kid, go ahead!' He said 'Kid, I'm for you.' He encouraged me. When he was away we wrote letters. I could tell him what I was going to do and he'd write back: 'Go ahead, kid. Good for you!'

I was fortunate I had a big brother, And he's still with me. And I still love him. I argue with him. Sometimes I think he's the stubbornest so and so I ever met in my life. I don't know what the hell I'd do without him."

Less than three months after Walt Disney World opened, at the age of seventy-eight, Roy Oliver Disney died on December 20, 1971, in the same hospital where his brother had died.

Walt was one of history's biggest dreamers, which probably makes Roy one of history's biggest dream makers. They were brothers first and business partners second. The two men, who helped bring so many of the best stories in family entertainment to life, actually created a pretty amazing story themselves.

The story of the Disney brothers is a wonderful tale of hard work, determination, and cooperation. The brothers needed each other to achieve their accomplishments. They showed us that we need to stick together and support our families through good times and bad.

As Walt once said: "The important thing is the family. If you can keep the family together—and that's the backbone of our whole business, catering to families—that's what we hope to do."

Today both Walt's and Roy's legacies lives on. Roy's son, Roy E. Disney, had a career as an executive at the company his father and uncle created. He passed away on December 16, 2009. Walt's daughter Diane opened the Disney Family Museum in San Francisco, California on October 1, 2009. The museum is a celebration of her father's life's work. Diane passed away on November 19, 2013. Walt's daughter Sharon passed away on February 16, 1993.

Walt's original theme park, Disneyland, still thrives today. The park Roy oversaw, Walt Disney World, is now the world's most visited theme park. Today the Disney property in Florida consists of four theme parks, two water parks, over thirty hotels, and hundreds of restaurants.

Walt's original dream of EPCOT was never realized. Walt Disney was really the only man who could ever bring that enormous project to life. However, with so many visitors to Walt Disney World each and every day, often times numbering over 100,000, it basically is a town of its own.

The small family business, founded in 1923, grew to so much more than the studio that created Mickey Mouse.

The company that bares the brothers' name now owns Marvel Entertainment, Pixar Animation Studios, and the iconic Star Wars franchise. Their products and entertainment are everywhere we look, and there are even Disney theme parks in Japan, France, Hong Kong, and China.

Not too bad for two farm boys from the Midwest!

Fun Facts About Disneyland

- The Disneyland Resort offers more than 8,500 different food items.
- Disneyland Resort guests consume approximately 350,000 apples each year. If stacked on top of each other, that many apples would reach 17 miles into the sky, or the height equivalent of 1,146 Sleeping Beauty Castles.
- If the 3,800,000 churros that are consumed each year at the Disneyland Resort were laid end-to-end, they would stretch 954 miles. That's enough churros to line the Disneyland Resort monorail track 382 times.
- Disneyland Resort guests consume 860,000 Mickey-shaped pretzels annually. That's enough each year to serve at least 29 pretzels to all 29,000 cast members at the Disneyland Resort.
- If the 2,600,000 hot dogs that are served each year were laid end-to-end, they would stretch 242 miles or the length of 11,208 Millennium Falcons.

- More than 300,000 pounds of bananas are consumed at the Disneyland Resort each year, which is approximately 130,000 individual bananas for Baloo from "The Jungle Book" to enjoy.
- Over the course of a given year, guests purchase more than 12 million kids meals, and parents typically choose the nutritious sides and beverages that Disney offers as the menu default option. Six out of 10 kids meals were served with the healthy options in 2016.
- More than 3,000 species of plants indigenous to 40 nations grow at the Disneyland Resort, making it one of the most extensive and diverse botanical locales in the western United States.
- The Mickey Mouse flower "portrait" at the Disneyland entrance is planted nine times a year. This flowerbed, a popular photo location, features 3,600 annuals in the face and 6,400 on the sides for a total of approximately 90,000 plants per year.
- The oldest living tree at the Disneyland Resort is a Mugho Pine that is only two feet tall. Guests will spot this tree, which is more than 150 years old, as they cruise on the Storybook Land Canal Boats.

Fun Facts About Walt Disney World

It's Not a Small World, After All . . . Covering nearly 40 square miles, Walt Disney World Resort is about the size of San Francisco or two Manhattan islands. Of the nearly 25,000 acres, a third is designated as conservation land.

A Cast of Thousands . . . more than 70,000 Cast Members in Central Florida to be more precise. That's how many people it takes to create the magic at the Vacation Kingdom. Not surprisingly, Walt Disney World Resort is the largest single-site employer in the United States.

What the Well-Dressed Mouse Will Be Wearing . . . depends entirely on the occasion. Mickey Mouse himself has more than 136 different sets of duds, ranging from a scuba suit to a tuxedo. Minnie Mouse's wardrobe contains more than 100 outfits, including everything from a cheerleader ensemble to evening gowns.

Suds 'R Us . . . If you were to wash and dry one load of laundry every day for 52 years, you'd clean as much a the folks at Walt Disney World Laundry do in a *single day*. The cast members there launder an average of 285,000 pounds each day. In addition, between 30,000 and 32,000 garments are dry-cleaned daily.

Who's Still Thirsty? . . . More than 75 million Cokes are consumed each year at Walt Disney World Resort along with 13 million bottles of water.

Ears to You . . . When laid end to end, there are enough of the famous "Mouse Ear" hats sold each year to stretch 175 miles or cover the head of every man, woman and child in Orange County, Fla. There are also enough Disney character T-shirts sold to put Mickey Mouse's smiling face on the chest of every resident of Montana.

Sign Here . . . If you stacked the number of standard autograph books sold annually, it would match the height of 200 Cinderella Castles. Add the Princess-style autograph books and, end to end, the books would reach 88 miles into space.

Gone But Not Forgotten . . . Walt Disney World Lost and Found is one busy place. Every day an average of 210 pairs of sunglasses are turned in and, since 1971, an estimated 1.65 million pairs of glasses have found their way into the "lost" bin. On an annual basis, Lost and Found cast members collect more than 6,000 cell phones, 3,500 digital cameras, 18,000 hats and 7,500 autograph books.

Curious Claims . . . According to long-time Lost and Found staffers, the most unusual items turned in have been a glass eye, a prosthetic leg and a potty trainer.

Each, incidentally, was claimed (but not by the same person).

Busman's Holiday . . . With nearly 400 buses, the Walt Disney World fleet is approximately the same size as that of St. Louis Metro Transit and larger than the bus fleet operated by the Los Angeles Department of Transportation.

Fly Me to the Moon . . . Since 1971, the total miles logged by Walt Disney World monorail trains would be equal to more than 30 round trips to the moon. One dozen new cars were put into service along the 14-mile beamway in 1990 as the original fleet received a well-deserved retirement.

Finger Food . . . More than 1.8 million pounds of turkey drumsticks are consumed every year in four Disney theme parks — Magic Kingdom, Epcot, Disney's Hollywood Studios and Disney's Animal Kingdom.

Room Roulette . . . If you wanted to stay in all of the guest rooms in all of the hotels and resorts currently open on Walt Disney World property, (at a rate of one per night) it would take decades.

Bloomin' Beauty . . . Nearly 12 percent of Walt Disney World property — an area equivalent to nearly 3,000 football fields — is devoted to gardens and maintained landscapes. That's 4,000 acres worth of beauty.

Well Grounded . . . Each year a horticulture staff plants 3 million bedding plants and annuals, and maintains millions of other plants including more than 4 million shrubs, 13,000 roses and more than 200 topiary.

A "Family" Tree . . . The "Liberty Oak," which is the focal point of the Liberty Square area in Magic Kingdom, is the proud parent of more than 500 young trees. They all started out as acorns harvested from the majestic oak.

Mow Miles Per Year . . . 450,000 mowing miles, to be exact — that's what it takes to maintain 2,000 acres of turf. For the record, those mower miles are the equivalent of 18 trips around Earth at the equator.

Bibliography

Gabler, N. (2007). Walt Disney: The triumph of the American Imagination(B). New York: Knopf.

Goldberg, A. (2016). The Disney Story (1st ed.). Philadelphia: Quaker Scribe.

The Walt Disney Family Museum. (n.d.). Retrieved from http://www.waltdisney.org/

The Official Disney Fan Club. (n.d.). Retrieved from https://d23.com/

Thomas, B., & Vosburgh, L. (1966). Walt Disney, magician of the movies. New York: Grosset & Dunlap.

Thomas, B. (1998). Building a company: Roy O. Disney and the creation of an entertainment empire. S.l.: Hyperion.

Thomas, B. (1981). The Walt Disney biography. London: Star Books.

About the Author

Aaron Goldberg is an alumnus of the University of Pennsylvania, having graduated with bachelor's and master's degrees in anthropology. He is the author of the best-selling books, *The Disney Story: Chronicling the Man, the Mouse and the Parks* and *The Wonders of Walt Disney World.*

Aaron and his book have been mentioned in stories about Disney in the Los Angeles Times and the Huffington Post. He's active on Twitter @aaronhgoldberg and has visited the Walt Disney World Resort more times than his wallet cares to remember!

Other Great Books by Aaron!

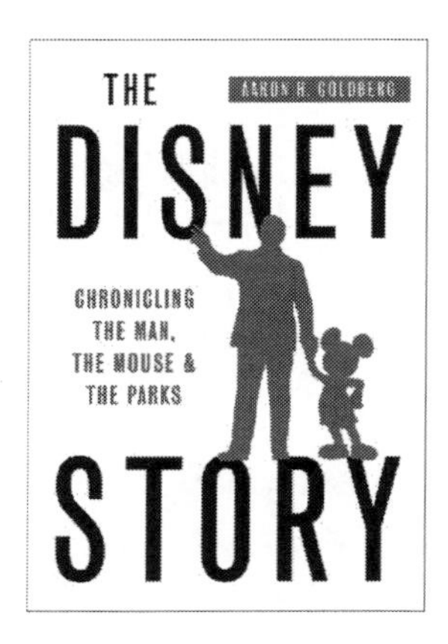

aaronhgoldberg.com

Made in the USA
Middletown, DE
25 February 2020